OPTIONS TRADING

Beginners Guide to Mastering Making Money With Options Trading

Table of Contents

Introduction

Increasing financial literacy has spurred more material regarding the once forbidden and feared area of trading in financial instruments. On top of that, it has engendered a necessity to cover the variety of opinions and strategies that have been tested and applied by traders in the industry.

However, the book should not be taken as a Rosetta Stone for upcoming traders, but as a guide into the basics of options trading. We hope that this serves its purpose and also that the reader will find the knowledge he or she is looking for.

As has been stressed in the book, the learner needs to acquaint himself first with the character of a prospective trader and later during the course of his learning the intuition of a master trader. This book is tuned to provide just that. This introductory path to professional trading will hopefully not only serve the apprentice but also the professional trader, who occasionally might find the need to refresh what he is already subconsciously aware of.

We hope that the reader will find its use and not only that, but also that he or she will be courageous to apply the skills advocated.

Chapter 1:
Options Trading Overview

Options have always been misconceived as an area of great risk and danger; however, this book will serve to destabilize this conception. In the United States, options have increasingly become very popular. Apart from being the preserve of institutions and companies, individual retail traders have taken to it. When starting out in the options business, one is always discouraged by the numerous warnings of great losses awaiting them. However; as it turns out, to succeed in the options business, one simply has to have a plan that works- a trading plan, that is. This trading plan has to be tuned to align to the goals intended- keeping the risks low and the profits maximized.

Every successful trader, like every successful person in any profession has to cultivate some traits that will function to make him better and more concise in his or her trading activities. The character of the individual, more than anything, makes the best traders- so, what area these character traits that suit the trading of stock options?

1) Patience

One of the most satisfying experiences for traders is making as much money as possible with every trade placed. Some are successful in this by the application of proper judgment whereas others are successful by the use of the appropriate skills needed and acquired through their journey as traders. Strategies in trading are developed over time, and so for one to master the skillset necessary for all good trades one has to take the time to develop the skills needed. When one is able to reject below-standard opportunities, then one can be assured and can satisfy himself with the conviction that he or she is getting there.

The question that one must ask himself is this: would he or she be comfortable undertaking brain surgery? If the answer is negative, then one should not think of approaching trading in the first place. Trading can be compared to such demanding tasks as surgery. Although in this case one does not lose his or another's life, one is placing his income (or in that case, his money) on the line. Nobody ever goes into a competition or nobody would want to lose something out of ignorance. The first step is just that- pruning ignorance. To do this, one first has to give it time- time to learn. A huge reflection that you are doing this is the fact that you are reading this book. For the first time traders, this is a huge step. In fact, this should be the most basic of the steps one would take in future after adopting the trade of options.

The second form of patience demanded is the patience during the trade itself. One has to be patient during the trading itself. All or most have had the experience of getting into an investment early even when they are not convinced of it being the best decision. There are plenty of challenges available on the internet, and equally in this book. Simplicity is the order of the game; in fact, simplicity has always been the order of the game. Regardless of the technique adopted by the trader, it is important that one wait for the right opportunity to present itself.

To make the most from options trading, one has to give oneself enough time to gain the experience, and then begin applying the principles after one learns to apply the skills learnt. Also, to add on the necessity of the virtue innate in patience, the value imposed on compounding must as well be adhered to. In terms of passages, if one is able to make a figure of one percent each week that translates to over sixty percent in a year's time. In this way, returns are allowed to accumulate and compounding takes over the rest of the job.

2) Perseverance

Having made the goal of becoming a successful trader, one has to stick to it. To do this and later avoid the chances of falling into disappointed it is necessary also that one sticks to realistic goals set in a realistic timeframe. This, as much as being a soft challenge to the apprentice, creates the motivation and the momentum of learning more as well as gaining experience.

3) Knowledge

Knowledge is acquired through the patience of the young trader and the application of the trading strategies in real markets. This is made possible in the current age by the diverse number of tools in the trading hemisphere. The internet as well makes it possible for real time acquisition of trading information to be applied by the learner.

This book allows for acquisition of knowledge on options and the application of that knowledge in real life. Learners in this course should focus on the retention of the values already discussed aside from focusing mainly on knowledge since the best traders have or try to align their skills with their character.

4) Honesty

The shortest thing that can be mentioned on honesty is that one should learn to take accountability of one's decisions and not blame others for anything.

5) Pre-Planning

Every trade must be pre-planned. One must know his or her maximum risk, maximum reward, break even points. One must go ahead and plan for their entry points and the exit point- whether to take profit or stop losses.

6) Discipline

The young trader must at all times stick to what he or she has already outlined as the methods he or she will use towards achieving the goals he intended to achieve. This means sticking to the deadlines where they appear and also adhering to the techniques of trading set forth before the real trading begins.

What is An Option?

An option, as the English connotation of the word implies, refers to the right- not the obligation, to buy or sell an asset at a fixed price before a pre-determinate date.

The phrases we have used to define an option have very important consequences. *The right, not the obligation* clearly implies that buying the option gives you the power to sell an underlying financial instrument. Therefore, when you buy an option you are not obligated to buy or sell the underlying financial instrument. The price one places in this transaction is the risk one incurs.

Selling an option on the other hand obliges one to buy from (with sold puts) or deliver (with sold calls) to the option buyer if he or she exercises the option. Selling options naked –for example, when one has not bought a position in the underlying instrument or an option to hedge against it- gives one an unlimited risk profile.

The fact that one is obliged to do something along with these trades is generally not preferable a position at any given time. Advanced traders; however, are in a better position taking the risk of dealing with naked options. From the above information, we conclude that:

1) The call buyer has the right but not the obligation to buy stock from the seller
2) The call seller is obliged to sell stock to call buyer if exercised
3) The put buyer; on the other hand, has the right to sell stock to the put seller
4) The put seller is obliged to buy stock from the put buyer if exercised

Benefits of Trading Options

There has been increased interest in the trade of options, with the increase in the number of literate people in the area of financial trade instruments. The majority of this cause of increase has been spurred by the internet and the penetration of diverse forms of media making professionals accessible to many groups of people. Furthermore, options are a cheaper option compared to the direct trade in the underlying stocks.

On the other hand, traders experienced in the options niche of the market have always used the advantage of options to hedge their portfolios, and also to take the advantage of market conditions that cannot be traded by the underlying stocks or the underlying futures.

1) Leverage

Option trading has the unique advantage of leveraging capital through the mechanism of a small amount of capital to control a larger piece of the underlying stock. One can and is able to control shares using just a fraction of the total value of shares at play. This means that for a small investment the profit is able to march a larger portion than the one it appears to be controlling on the surface.

2) Flexibility

Options provide a very flexible tool since they are available for a wide array of assets including stocks, stocks, futures and other markets such as currencies. One can buy or sell options with a wide variety of strike prices and various contract expiration periods. Stocks and indices offer LEAPS, which are long duration options, giving one flexible expiration dates that can be years away.

Out of the uniqueness of their structures, options can be purchased in many differing combinations to take advantage of the existing market conditions. Option strategies can also be created to suit rising or declining markets, markets with no price movements, explosive markets where the direction of the market is unclear or even as a hedge to protect profits.

When one trades the underlying asset, one profits then from the directional movement. However, with the case of options one is able to benefit from diverse market conditions, making trade in these very attractive to the entities involved.

3) Limited Risks- Unlimited Profits

The maximum loss one can incur after the purchase of an option contract is the amount one paid for the option contract. On the other hand, there is no cap on the profits one stands to benefit. This limited risk unlimited profit profile makes it attractive for investors who want to know what their risk potential is with any trade they place.

Options also provide a way for one to limit the way investment is exposed to risk. Volatility, time, interest and the asset price are some of the factors that can affect the risk of an option position. However, option strategies can be created or adjusted to limit one's risk for the factors when the market is going against one. One is also able to protect his or her portfolio through the hedging of stocks or futures by purchasing options to protect one's holdings from adverse movements of assets. Individual options can be used to hedge individual assets or index options can be used to hedge a basket of stocks in just a single transaction.

4) Guaranteed Contract Performance

An option holder is able to look to the system created by OCC's Rules which includes the brokers and Clearing Members involved in a particular option transaction and to certain funds held by OCC - rather than to any particular option writer for performance. Prior to the existence of option exchanges and OCC, an option holder who wanted to exercise an option depended on the ethical and financial integrity of the writer or his brokerage firm for performance. Furthermore, there was no convenient means of closing out one's position prior to the expiration of the contract. OCC, as the common clearing entity for all exchange traded option transactions, resolves these difficulties. Once OCC is satisfied that there are matching orders from a buyer and a seller, it severs the link between the parties. In effect, OCC becomes the buyer to the seller and the seller to the buyer. As a result, the seller can buy back the same option he has written, closing out the initial transaction and terminating his obligation to deliver the underlying stock or exercise value of the option to OCC, and this will in no way affect the right of the original buyer to sell, hold or exercise his option. All premium and settlement payments are made to and paid by OCC.

Types of Options

A *call* is an option to buy. A put is an option to sell. This is therefore interpreted as:

- A call option is in fact the right, not the obligation to buy an asset at a fixed price before a date already predetermined
- A put option; on the other hand, is the right and not the obligation to sell an asset at a price fixed before a date already predetermined

There can be either American style or European style types of calls or puts.

While American style options allow the option buyer to exercise the option at any time before its date of expiry, European style options do not allow the buyer to exercise the options before the expiry date. In this sense, American style options are more popular than their European counterparts, reason being for its flexibility in allowing traders the liberty of selling even before the expiry date of the options. This also makes the American style options more valuable that their European counterparts.

As a rule; however, stock options are normally American style whereas futures options are normally European style.

Exercise (or Strike) Price

This refers to the fixed price at which the stock can be exercised. If one therefore buys a call option at a price of 50, then in actual practice this interprets as the right to buy the asset at the price of $50.

However, in the real world- acting out of rationality, one exercises the right to buy this option only when its value increases beyond the $50. In this case, one would have surely made a profit from exercising his right. Otherwise, there would be no point since this would mean purchasing a stock at a price lower than the actual price one is paying for.

Expiration Date

As mentioned before, this is the date the option expires. At the date of expiration, the call option's value is worth only the price of the asset minus the stock price, and at expiration, the put option's value is worth the strike price minus the price of the asset.

In the case of US equity monthly options, the expiration dates fall on the Saturday after the third Friday of each month. Weekly options have gained a lot in popularity, but still not quite as actively traded as the traditional monthly options.

We shall then consider the topics of intrinsic value and time value.

The Valuation of Options

Options have a value, as has already been mentioned, the only difference being that their value is totally separate from the stock they underlie and hence from which they are derived (hence the name derivatives). In themselves, their value can be split into two parts: intrinsic and time value.

Intrinsic value refers to that part of the option's value that is in the money. Time value, on the other hand, refers to the remainder of the option's value. Out of the money options have no intrinsic value, and their price will solely be based on the time left until expiration and the price of the underlying asset.

Hence:

a) A call is ITM (in the money) when the underlying asset price is greater than the strike price.
b) A call is OTM (out of the money) when the underlying asset price is less than the strike price.
c) A call is ATM (at the money) when the underlying asset price equals the strike price

Put options; on the other hand, work the opposite way:

a) A put is ITM when the underlying asset price is less than the strike price
b) OTM when the underlying asset price is actually greater than the strike price

c) ATM when the strike price and the asset price are on the same level

Why Trade Options?

The main advantage that comes with the trade of options is the fact that one can own a large amount of stock for a small amount of money- especially with call options. Call options are always cheaper than the underlying asset and put options usually are.

Options are generally more volatile than the instruments underlying them and investors tend to get more *bangs for their buck* or more action. This can lead to danger; but, astonishingly it can also lead to more security. One can also get more flexibility in their trading and even enjoy the ability to make profit when one is in ignorance on the direction the stock is heading towards.

Investors with portfolios can set up measures protective of their assets in the event of a market downturn. It is also very possible and indeed, feasible, for one to set himself in a position one is able to make profit without stopping at it- perhaps not a huge margin of profit, but profit nonetheless.

Factors Influencing an Options Premium

Seven factors influence directly or indirectly the pricing of an option. We have to analyze once more the definition of an option to understand in depth how these factors actually have an influence in the pricing of an option.

An option, as already discussed, is defined as:

- Right, not the obligation
- To buy or to sell
- An asset
- At a price that is fixed
- Before a predetermined date

From the definition, therefore:

- *To buy or to sell is* interpreted as the type of option one is dealing with- whether a call or a put
- *Underlying asset* and its *own price* affect the option premium
- *At a fixed price* The strike price affects the option premium
- *Before a predetermined date* The expiration date and the time value affect the option premium

There are three other major influences on option pricing

- Volatility
- Risk free rate of interest
- Dividends payable

Risk Profile Charts for Call Options

Since the above has highlighted the valuation of the stock, we have then to look at the risk profile of a put option. A put option- it should be clear, is the right to sell an asset. This suggests, forming a picture in the mind- that the graph of a put option goes in the opposite direction to that of the call option.

Buying Is a Right

- Buying an option, gives you the right to sell the instrument underlying the option be it a share or anything for that matter
- When one buys a put option, he or she is not obligated to sell the instrument the option is attached to
- One's risk when an option is bought is simply the price one pays for it
- One's reward in the trade of options is simply the price that one pays for it

Selling (Naked) Imposes the Obligation

- Selling a put option, as discussed, obliges one to buy the option from the option buyer. When one sells a put, one has sold the right to sell to the person who bought that put

- One is given an unlimited risk profile when one sells a naked option
- Combining with the fact that one is obliged to do something, this makes it not a preferred position for one to put oneself in

Chapter 2:
Into the Trading Sphere

The components of an on-screen option price are as follows:

1) The underlying instrument
2) The expiration date of the option
3) The symbol of the option
4) The exercise strike price of the option
5) The ask/bid price of the option
6) The option volume on that particular day
7) The option interest of a specific option

Options Contracts

Listed stock options are traded in contracts, each contract differing according to the jurisdiction. The contracts in the United States represent for shares each represent 100 shares whereas in the United Kingdom, each represents 1000 shares for each contract. Therefore, a United States equity of 1.45

invites one to pay a total of 1.45 * 100 shares. One such contract therefore grants one the privilege of owning one hundred shares of the stock underlying.

The table below underlines the set of securities represented by a single contract under different markets:

Option Exchanges

The United States has more than ten exchanges, making it the mecca in the world of derivatives. As more and more retail traders increase, the trading of options equally increases every month.

Options Expiry Dates

Every option has an expiration date normally specified as a month, although there are also weekly options. Trading of options in the United States normally ends on Friday, although the trader can exercise the option on the final Saturday.

Strike Prices

In the United States, option strike prices would start at $2.50 then rising in $2.50 increments up to $25 and then later increment slowly until they reach the 200 dollar mark. At $200 they would go up in $10 increments. While many stocks of little liquidity normally adhere to this structure for their options, normally the larger cap stocks have more strikes and weekly operations.

Option Ticker Symbols

Option symbols changed to a more logical and more robust form in the year 2010. Just like individual stocks, individual options have individual ticker symbols. This identifies the underlying stock, the strike price and the type of option.

Margin

The margin requirement is the amount of cash and deposits required on deposits to cover the risk the broker incurs. A margin account therefore ensures adequate security for the stocks being traded- this being necessary for those traders who sell short, sell naked, or even engage in the trading of net credit spreads. Margin therefore works as a leverage mechanism with stock trades. With option trades; however, it is used to ensure adequate collateral as already mentioned.

When one buys shares, one can either pay in cash or use a margin account- in which case one uses (borrows) up to only half the percentage of the share price. The *maintenance margin* is set to ensure the balance in the account never spills up to a negative figure. In the past, this has been set up to a value of 25 percent of the value of the shares, even though this usually varies.

When a trader buys a put or a call option, he or she would be forced to pay in full the purchase price. One cannot buy the options on margin since they already contain significant leverage and therefore buying them on margin would raise the leverage levels to unacceptable levels. In this case, margin relates to collateral requirements.

Selling options naked means that there does not exist covering trades to hedge the risk of the naked sale. The risk of selling calls and puts should be recalled and the diagonal lines continue uninterrupted on the downside. This uninterrupted downside is what must therefore be protected. It follows then that when one sells naked call or put options, one needs to maintain funds in a margin as collateral. In this way, the option writer does not default on the obligation if the option buyer exercises the right. The size of margin varies depending on the trade entered into.

When one sells short or trades a net credit spread, and money is deposited into the subject's account by the trade, there is still a contingent liability risk which is covered by the sufficient funds left on deposit in one's account.

These funds can be represented in either cash or marginable securities. A marginable security is an asset deemed by the brokerage to be secure enough to stand as collateral against one's risk on the trade. A blue chip stock would pass as marginable security, while low priced stocks with little trading history, low volumes of trade and high volatility cannot be accepted as such.

Placing Your Trade

It is imperative that one will place option trades through an online platform. One point to remember; however, is that since option prices are not always clean, one has to place limit orders particularly on spreads. This ensures that orders are filled at one's specified price or not filled at all.

Chapter 3:
Types of Orders

Market Order

With this types of orders, one ensures through the stock broker that orders are placed at the best price in the market at any particular time.

Limit Order

With limit orders, one can buy only if the share can fall to a certain price or lower or in the other case, one can sell only if the share rises to a certain price or even higher.

With options, limits are recommended, particularly in the case of spreads and combination trades. The reason for this is that the bid or ask spread prices can fluctuate dramatically and often not in one's favor so this makes it a lot better if one specifies the price.

Stop Loss or Sell Stop

At this point, one sells only if the shares fall below a particular price. Sell stop is usually placed below the current price. However, one can choose to increase the stop loss if the share happens to rise.

Buy Stops

This is where one buys only on condition that the share has reached or has exceeded a certain predetermined price. This is the opposite of a limit order where one buys a stock after it has fallen to a particular price.

Buy Stop

This is where one buys a stock after it has reached or exceeded a particular price. This is the opposite of a limit order, where one buys a stock after it has fallen to a particular price. A buy stop is appropriate and fits a situation one one expects a stock to rise beyond a resistance level or bounce up from a supported level.

Two types of buy stocks exist:

- *Buy stop with limit*: In this case, the buy only occurs when the stock is between two configured prices
- *Buy stop with limit and stop loss*: In this case, the buy is placed between two prices and sell if the price is below a particular configured price

Time Limits with Trade Orders

Good Till Cancelled

In this case, the order is valid unless and until one cancels it or in the other scenario, until it is filled. In this case, a limit order GTC authorizes the broker to buy the stock at a particular price or lower than the price configured for that purpose. It may be that particular day or any other day occuring in the future when the stock is selling at a particular amount until one has bought the requisite number of shares.

A point of caution is that every trader needs to be very careful with these orders since they normally do not go to the top of the priority list of the floor traders' priorities.

Day Only

In this case, the order is cancelled if not filled by the end of the day. The positive about this is that it encourages the day traders to deal. If this is not the case by the end of the trading day, no commision would be paid to them. Consequently, as can be inferred, the trader then makes it his or her priority to trade so that they can earn commision on the trades placed. With some traders, stop limit orders can only be placed on a day basis and so these are recurrent on each day.

Week Only

As the name suggests, in this case the order is cancelled if it is not filled by the week's end.

Fill Kill

If not placed immediately, the order is cancelled. Fill kill therefore is the order with maximum priority compared to the orders already discussed above. This type of order is specifically for the purpose of capturing the attention of the traders but if it is a limit order, then it needs to be made realistic.

All or None

In this case, either the entire order is filled or none is filled at all. Generally, this is never a good idea given that all trades are not filled at once because there has to be both a buyer and a seller for a trade to occur. Also, another conflict bound to occur is that most of the times they are not aiming for the same sizes in terms of trade. Therefore, if one wants to be sure of getting filled, one should avoid going for all or none.

Always have a stop in mind whenever making a trade. It is common for some people to trade without placing a stop order to their brokers. This is illegal or unacceptable at the very least but the very best of trained traders are always sure to have a stop in mind whenever they are entering a trade. If not the case, then it is necessary to have a mental stop order in mind, so that one can act on it when the limit is reached.

Where one chooses to place a stop is a matter idiosyncratic, but the general and acceptable norm is to place the stop beyond the appropriate support or the appropriate resistance area. Also, in most cases, when one places a stop it is generally recommended that one places it or bases it not on the option price but using the actual stock price as a template for the same.

Whipsaws

This occurs when a price changes direction suddenly almost as common as twice or more. Although it has been observed in the previous sections the need and the usefulness of using stops, it should be mentioned that whipsaws create a very dangerous position where one is likely to be stopped out. In such a case, one automatically loses a winning position. To put this into perspective, assume that one buys a stock for a total of fifty dollars. In the course of the day and in quick movement, the stock then depreciates to less than fifty dollars. A stop order protects one from getting losses in this scenario. But; on the other hand, and in equally quick succession the stock may rise to a higher figure than the initial fifty dollars. This means that one loses a winning position not particularly from the effect of the whipsaws, but also from the restriction of the stop order. This is the danger of whipsaws, in collaboration with stop orders. As has been seen, this might lead to a dangerous position for the trader.

Leverage and Gearing

The two words above are used frequently in the financial sphere. In terms of a company's financial structure, they refer to the ration of a company's borrowing over assets owned. In general, the higher a company's gearing, the higher its return on equity. A higher gearing interprets as greater risk to a company because if fixed and variable costs are not exceeded by turnover, the company's creditors might be able to foreclose the company by calling in the loans.

In the options world however, the words carry a clearly different meaning. In the options world, as has already been seen, options carry a high leverage because a small percentage change move in the underlying assets can mean a very high change in the corresponding options.

How Does Leverage with Options Work?

Example:

Take a company A, whose stock price is at the time $20. One decides to buy a call option with an exercise price e of $.25, with the call option in turn costing $1. An option has two parts to its value:

- Time value
- Intrinsic value

In this case, unless the stock price rises to a figure above twenty five dollars, there would be no intrinsic value since the exercise price is at twenty five dollars. There would be intrinsic value, however, if the stock rises to above twenty five dollars.

For the same example, assume no change for the time value element. So, it the stock price rises to a figure such as 30, what intrinsic value does the option carry? The answer is the difference between the stock price of 30 and the price at $25.

Therefore, from the above case, it should be noted that in most of the cases, the value of the call option must be at least five dollars. The company share price from twenty dollars to thirty dollars indicates an increase of 50%. However, this is an increase of upto 400% considering that the option premium has risen from 1 to 5.

It should be noted that leverage works the other way too. If the stock depreciates, then this is a loss of gain for the trader.

Introduction to Delta

What has been observed in the latter example is a case of delta. This is measured as a ratio of the change in option price divided by the change in the underlying asset price.

As observed, when a call option becomes in the money, the delta increases. From this, it can be deduced that the higher the delta, the faster the option price moves compared to the stock price. On the other hand, buying out of the money options is not the solution. One reduces his or her chances of success since the change in option price is much slower, making it more difficult to make profit.

There are ways one can protect oneself against delta by using combination or spread trades. These trades' intention is to reduce the risk of exposure to delta by bringing the delta value close to zero, so that one is not exposed to these wild swings on the downward direction while also maintaining one's probability of success. This is what is referred to as delta neutral trading.

It should be clarified that delta neutral does not imply no risk at all. This is not some sort of nirvana. It should be pointed out; however, that it can reduce risk in certain circumstances but with particular techniques mastered over the course of time.

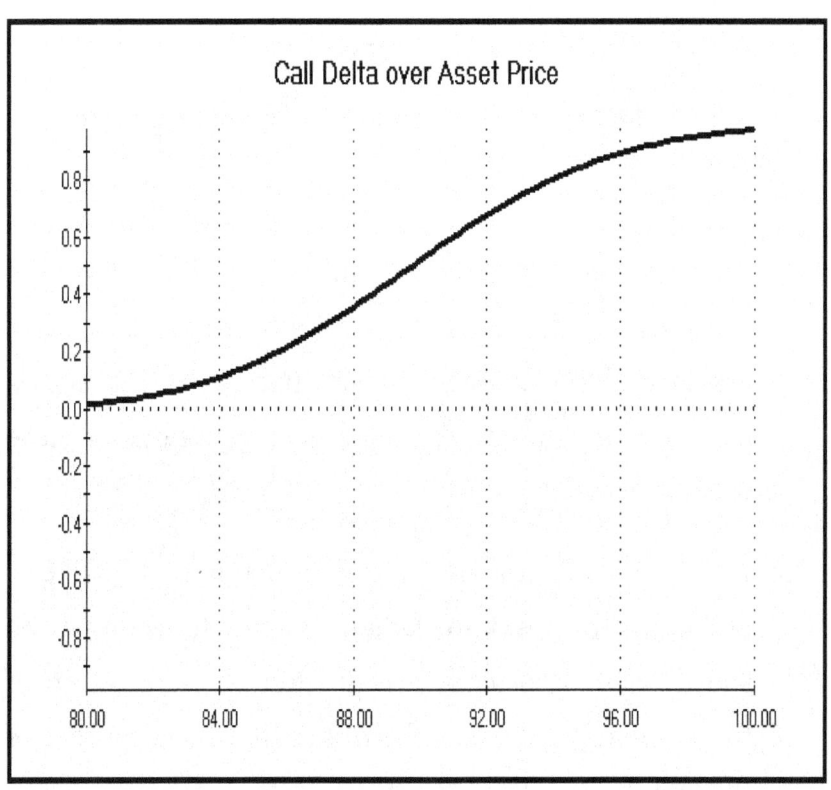
Call Delta over Asset Price

Chapter 4:
Fundamental Analysis

This is the procedure applied in the study of companies with regard to their revenues, profits, assets and borrowings. Most financial ratios one is bound to encounter are simply manipulations of these variables.

It is necessary for any trader to acquaint himself or herself with this knowledge because the company's share price is basically a reflection of the position of the company in terms of profitability. If the profits of the company are observed to grow year after year, then that company is ideal to invest in, provided one is optimistic that this growth will not come to an end soon enough.

Stock prices are basically driven by expectations, and expectations by sentiment. Sentiment on the other hand, is normally influenced by such factors as the news on a particular company and also and very importantly, the history of the particular company. News encompasses the company not only within its jurisdiction but also outside of its jurisdiction hence implying both within the borders the company falls and outside the borders the company falls.

Past History and Management

What the company does, how it has performed in the past and the track record of the team encompassing management of the company are all important towards successful determination of the performance or the likely performance of the company. Many investors have come to base their investment decisions majorly on the performance of the management over a couple of years they have been involved in running the company.

News and Results

News, unlike the common parlance, in this section or for the benefit of the trader, involves the larger economy, the sector of the stock and the company itself not forgetting the world at large and the factors influencing its direction including politics and other volatile areas of the modern world.

Cases such as political turmoil or increase in the cost of energy. These factors might impact the company directly, leading to higher costs of production or in the optimistic mind lower the costs of production in turn maximizing profits. Such factors as inflation also serve to impact the prices of stocks by creating particular sentimentsl; which, as we have observed change the direction of markets and stock prices as well.

The results of a company's earnings reflect the performance of the company in question. These earnings are published during unique periods of the company's financial year with the United States companies expected to publish these every quarter whereas the United Kingdom mandating the publication of these financial statements at the end of every half financial year.

Sentiment and Expectation

It is common belief that markets are driven by emotions, but to what extent is this the case? There have been cases of young companies being valued upward of a billion dollars- what does information tell us about the trend of markets?

Other times, it may be surprising that companies with big profiles and a wide base as Coca-Cola get panned while low index companies do not experience such measures. In this case, expectations of the market on the company plays a very crucial role in directing the prices of the stock. It is surprising how inaccurate expectations can come to be. Expectations can be biased, it must be noted, since various factors come into play. Analysts may favor companies they are affiliated to whether directly or indirectly through such activities as the company they work for and their company doing business together and so on. Therefore, the young trader must be advised against following recommendations blindly.

In most cases, growth companies- while at first encompassing and engendering great expectations from prospective investors, when in fact from the history of other companies that have been traded longer on the exchanges, their price to earnings ratio regresses to the norm over a period of time.

The Wider Economy

In terms of analyzing the economy, a top down approach is preferred. The country and the wider economic atmosphere is analyzed in this case. That is, one looks at how the general economy is performing before getting to the individual companies one plans to invest money in. How good is the economy performing? What are its prospects and what are its potential threats? These are some of the questions one must answer when evaluating a particular economic jurisdiction.

There are key figures all traders must be acquainted with in relation to economics before one gets into the business of trading.

Indicators to Watch in the United States

Consumer Price Index (CPI)

This is the most widely cited inflation indicator and is used as a reference point when measuring the price of goods and services purchased in an economy. The figures relating to the consumer price index are often released at about half past eight in the morning on the thirteenth day of every month in the country.

The Report on Employment

This report is comprised of two surveys: the Household survey and the Establishment Survey. The household survey encompasses about sixty thousand households whereas the Employment Report encompasses about three hundred and seventy five thousand businesses. These are released at the same time as the consumer price index, although not on the same day but on the first Friday of every month. The details concerning these can be accessed at *http://stats.bls.gov/news.release/empsit.htm*

Gross Domestic Product

The fundamental components of the GDP are consumption, investment, net exports, government acquisitions and inventories.

On the third day of the fourth week of the first month of the new quarter, the figures relating to the GDP of the country are released.

Building Permits and Housing Starts

These are measures of the number of housing units that have begun construction at the beginning of each month; and by consequence, for that month. Start is a term referring to the excavation of the foundation for the purposes of construction and is mainly tied to residential buildings. These are led by Building Permits. Building Permits precede housing starts since they are prerequisite for construction to begin. Since Permits are not a requirement in every region in the United States, Starts provide a better insight into the information relating to these.

These statistics are released on the sixteenth day of each month, with respect to the data relating to the month prior. More details on these can be found at www.census.gov/ftp/pub/indicator/www/housing.html

National Association of Purchasing Managers

This report concerns purchasing managers and is calculated by way of a weighted average of various items including new orders, production, employment, inventories, delivery times, prices and export as well as import orders. Although the report covers the manufacturing sector only, it is seen as a major indicator of other economic releases.

The figures of the report are released in the morning of the first business day of each month with respect, as well, to the previous month's data. More details concerning the report can be found at: www.napm.org/public/rob/lastrob1/html

Producer Price Index

The PPI, being a measure of inflation, indicates the prices of goods at the wholesale level.

The figures regarding the PPI are released on the eleventh day of each month, with regard to data relating to the previous month.

Retail Sales

This report gives insight into the changes of consumer demands and is analyzed excluding data for the automobile, food and gasoline industries. Retail sales measure the total receipt of retail stores. The figures also exclude spending on services, which make up over half of the total consumption. The total personal consumption figures are often made available two weeks after the retail sales figures are published.

These figures are published in the morning of the thirteenth day of each month.

A complete view of the economic calendar can be found at: http://biz.yahoo.com/c/e.html

Bonds

Bonds are under the group of fixed income securities. These come in the form of T-bills which are issued by the government and bonds, which are issued by corporations. The amount of money bonds generate each year is fixed, hence the name of the category they belong. This is independent of events that occur during the period the bond is sold. The coupon handed out to the bond holder obliges an interest payment by the issuer.

Corporate bonds are issued for the purposes of raising money. These also carry higher interest rates as compared to T-bills since there is a much higher risk of the company going bankrupt. Both of these classes of bonds can be traded on the open market.

Basics of the Bond

- As already mentioned, bonds are debt instruments obliging the issuer to pay a fixed rate of interest with respect to the amount raised by the bond
- They are issued at *par value,* requiring the lender to receive from the borrower the amount lent at the end of the term of the bond
- The amount of interest the bondholder receives is what is referred to as the coupon rate, usually expressed as a percentage of the par value of the bond
- At maturity, the principal amount is redeemed by the bond-issuing company

- In the bond market, the interest rate is determined as well by the size of the company since established companies are more stable than those that have not yet established themselves
- The prices of bonds vary depending on the open market

The rules for traders to keep in mind in the bond market include the following:

- A strong bond market indicates that the prices of bonds are higher, the yield lower and the stock market is stronger
- A weak bond market indicates that bond prices are lower, the bond yields are higher and the stock market is weaker
- Where bond yields are greater than 6.75%, the stock market may suffer since yields are that much better than in bonds
- Where bond yields are lower than 3.5% the stock market may become stronger

since the bond yields are too low for an acceptable return

However, a point of caution is that not all these work at all times.

Supply and Demand

Economics is dictated by the rules of supply and demand therefore the prices of products and even stocks indicate the direction and can give a clue of the nature of supply or the nature of demand.

The basic rules of supply and demand are as stated below:

- *When the demand outstrips the supply, the prices go up.* This occurs when supply is confined or restricted yet the demand is growing very fast, even exponentially.
- *When demand drops relative to the supply, the prices go down.* Contrary to the previous scenario, when there is excess in the market and there happens

to be less demand for what is available, then the prices of those goods or services will ultimately drop

Rules, as has been indicated above, are not immune from misinterpretation or from being nothing but myths. It is not always that the cases presented above manifest as truth. This has been experienced in various sectors, including the real estate business. Just because masses believe something to be true, it is not always necessarily the case.

Market Direction

One should strive to understand the directions markets are taking, but not overstep by trying to predict them. Making a prediction is different from anticipation and recognition. Various tools and software products are available in the market for the recognition of the prevailing market direction at any given time.

Being able to interpret market direction provides the trader with a huge advantage over those who cannot predict the direction of that market. For this reason, it is necessary not only for traders to speculate without being extravagant, but also to learn the patterns common in a particular market at a particular time considering that most of these patterns are actually recurrent. Patterns are common in the trading sphere and it is imperative that traders be acquainted to them at all costs. The best traders in the financial markets have come to appreciate the value of interpreting markets and understanding the general pattern they tend to adopt. This is necessary for the aspiring traders as well, and should be mastered with all patience if one is to be successful in mistaking or placing unsupervised bets.

Option Strategies

For any trader in the options business, it is necessary to understand the various options strategies available for his or her application of the same. These strategies are often created using a combination of the four basic option positions: long call, short call, long put and short put. These strategies can provide, for the trader, opportunities in rising, declining, active and stagnant markets and even creating the opportunity for profit when no one is aware of the direction of the market. Through the effective combination of the different option contract months, strike prices and the number of contracts traded an option strategy can be created to take advantage of almost any market action or condition.

a) A call purchase is a long call, which is often a bullish or a very bullish position. The call purchase strategy benefits from an increase in the price of an underlying asset. Buying calls is an bullish strategy that can be used as replacement for the outright purchase of the underlying stock. The figure below illustrates this:

Market bias	Bullish
Risk	Premium Paid
Potential Reward	Unlimited
Premium	Paid in full at purchase- no margin calls

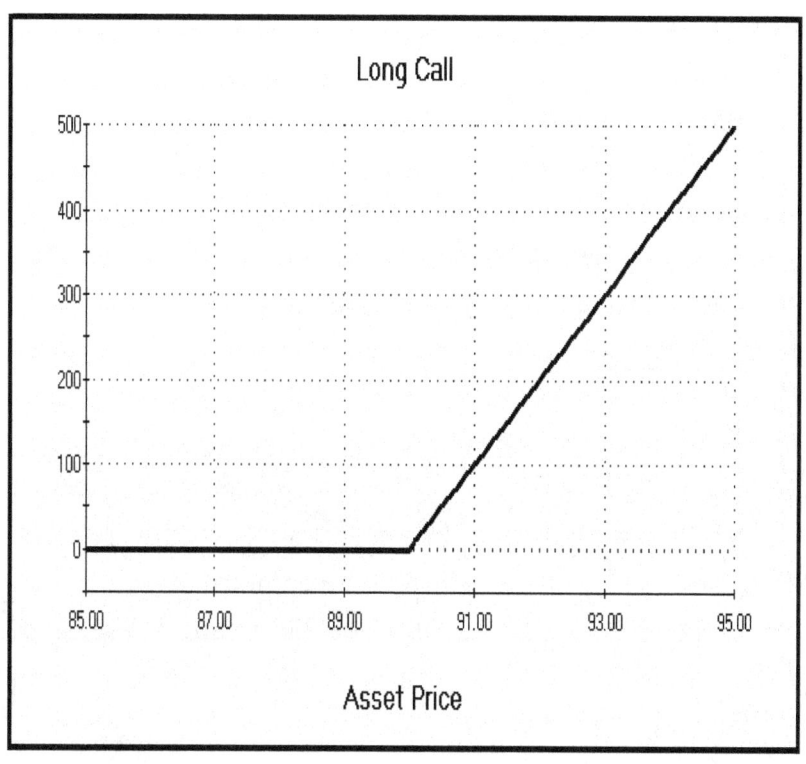

Long Call

b) A put purchase, on the other hand, is a very bearish position. The risk for the holder is limited to the premium paid for the option. The reward is unlimited to an underlying price of 0. The put purchase strategy, contrary to the first, benefits from the decrease in the price of the asset that underlies it. They are used if one is bearish on the asset underlying. They can therefore be used as an alternative to shorting the asset underlying. This purchase can also be used to protect a position that is at the time held position by locking in a selling price. Consider the table below

Market Bias	Bearish
Risk	Premium Paid
Potential Reward	Limited to difference between strike price and 0; less premium paid
Premium	Paid in full at purchase. No margin calls

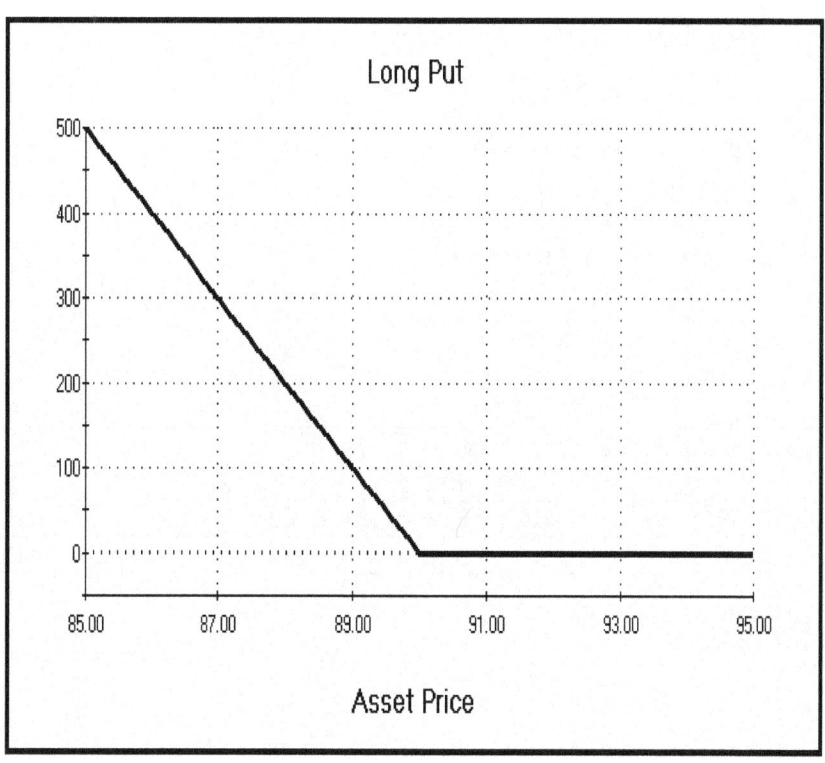

Writing a call is a slightly bearish or neutral position. The trader who executes the strategy is called the writer. It should be noted that the risk inherent in naked call writing can be high to the extreme and always carries margin requirements. In this strategy, the reward is normally limited to the premium received for selling the call option. The risk in this case is unlimited. This strategy is used if one is bearish on the underlying asset and normally to collect the premium when a trader or an investor feels the call option contract will expire without any worth or in other cases, will end up being worse than the premium received.

Market Bias	Bearish
Risk	Unlimited
Potential Reward	Premium received
Premium	Premium received; subject to margin calls

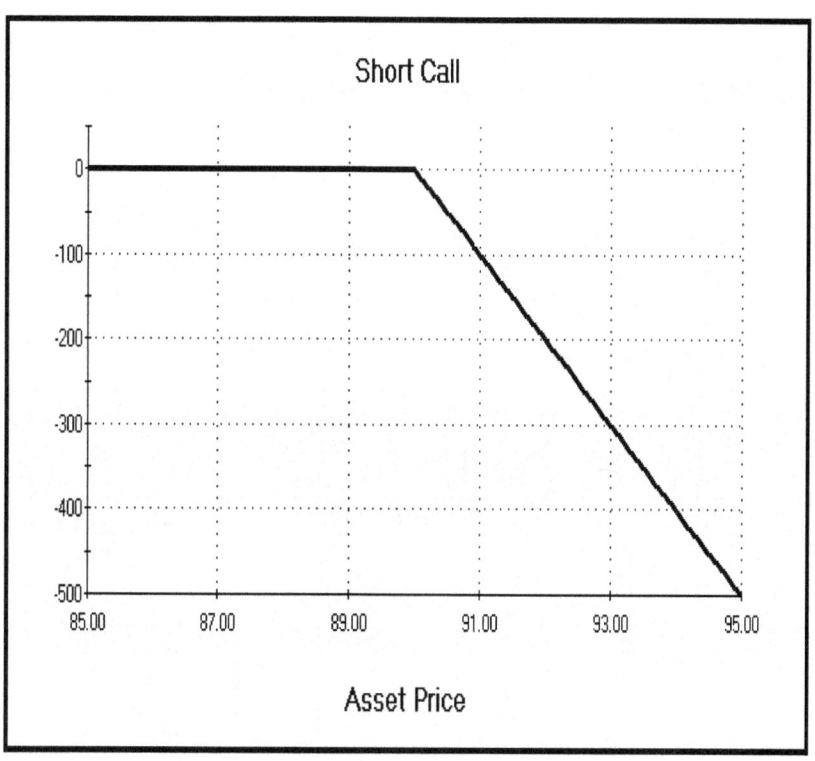

Short Call

c) Writing a short put involves or is usually associated with a bullish position. This strategy normally involves one writing a short put with an accompanying obligation to purchase a fixed number of the underlying asset from the holder on or before a particular time. The executor of this strategy is called the writer. The inherent risk in a naked put carries margin requirements since it can turn out to be extremely high. The table below illustrates this:

Market Bias	Bullish
Risk	Limited to difference between strike price and 0, less premium received
Potential Reward	Premium received
Premium	Premium received; subject to margin calls

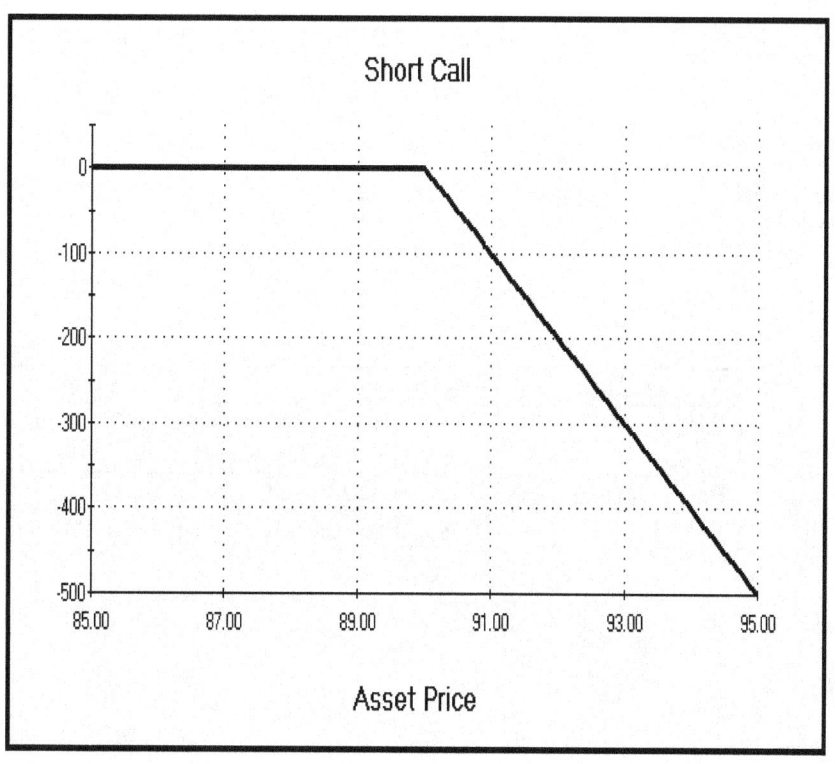

Short Call

Asset Price

d) Writing a short put involves or is usually associated with a bullish position. This strategy normally involves one writing a short put with an accompanying obligation to purchase a fixed number of the underlying asset from the holder on or before a particular time. The executor of this strategy is called the writer. The inherent risk in a naked put carries margin requirements since it can turn out to be extremely high. The table below illustrates this:

Market Bias	Bullish
Risk	Limited to difference between strike price and 0, less premium received
Potential Reward	Premium received
Premium	Premium received; subject to margin calls

Combining Legs into Strategies

General Option Spread Strategy Theory

The four strategies discussed above can now be used as the basic building blocks to create complex option strategies referred to as spreads. The advantage of spreads is that they can be applied to most marketing conditions.

An option spread position is an option position with two or more different option contracts or legs, in combination. Normally, a spread is composed of buying and writing different option types, strike prices or expiration dates in order to take advantage of some market position or even to increase the leverage of capital. when one combines writing options with buying options, the options one buys covers the options one writes thereby reducing or even eliminating a margin requirement.

Any time one creates or opens an option spread position with a debit, the debit of the position normally refers to the maximum amount one can lose on the position. On the other hand, when one creates or opens an option spread position with a credit, the credit normally refers to the maximum gain on the position which is normally accompanied by a margin requirement equal to the maximum loss of the position.

The price of the underlying asset at the strike price of the options one is selling is normally referred to the maximum gain point of a spread position, whereas the maximum loss price point is at the strike price of the options one is buying.

Finally, it is an important reminder to note that the maximum profit or the maximum loss of any spread position is only achieved on the date of expiry of the options, when the options that make up the strategy are only worth the difference of the spread- which is also referred to as the intrinsic value.

Covered Call

When one writes or sells a call against the current stock position, the result is what is referred to as a covered call. This basically entails owning a particular number of shares or contracts on the stock underlying and then following that by writing call options in the correct ratio.

The premium received in the call option is the reward one ultimately receives and on top of that any asset price movement up to the strike price of the sold option. Writers of covered calls normally prefer the stock to remain as close as possible to, but always below, the strike of the option sold for maximum profit since the option sold would then expire worthless.

Market Bias	Moderately Bullish
Risk	Asset price of 0, less premium received
Potential reward	Difference between price paid and option strike price plus premium received
Premium	Asset must be paid for, or margin. If margined then subject to asset margin calls

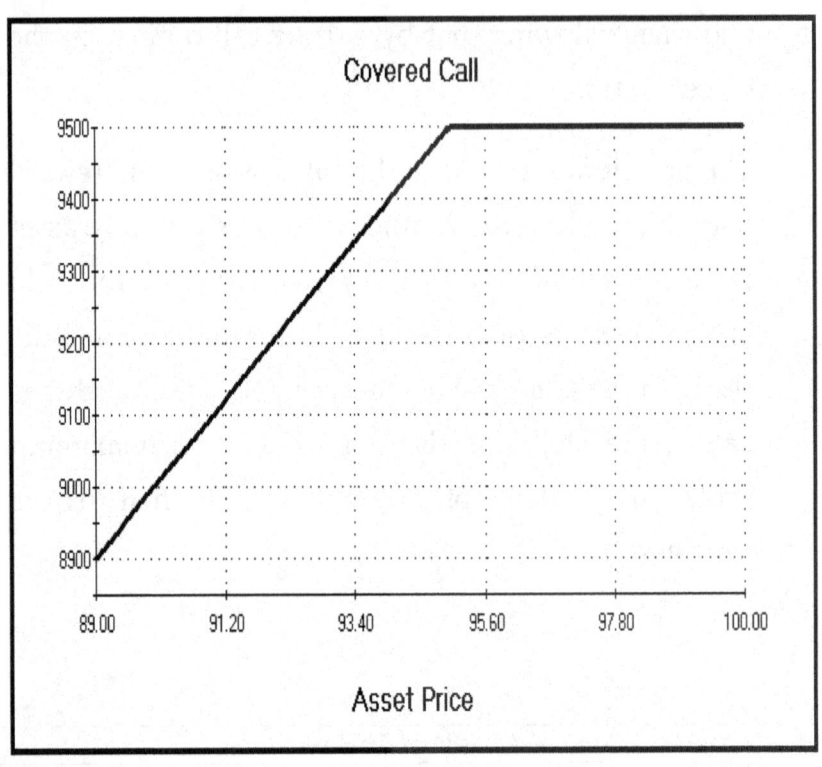

Debit Call Spread

This involves the purchase of one or more calls and the sale of an equal number of calls with a higher strike price. In case of a rise in the asset price, the long leg should be able to create a profit greater than the loss on the short leg. In case of a decline in the asset price, the net premium paid for the spread would always be smaller than a long call position alone.

Market Bias	Moderately bearish
Premium	Net premium paid at purchase; not subject to margin calls
Potential Reward	Difference in strike prices, less premium paid
Risk	Net premium paid (debit)

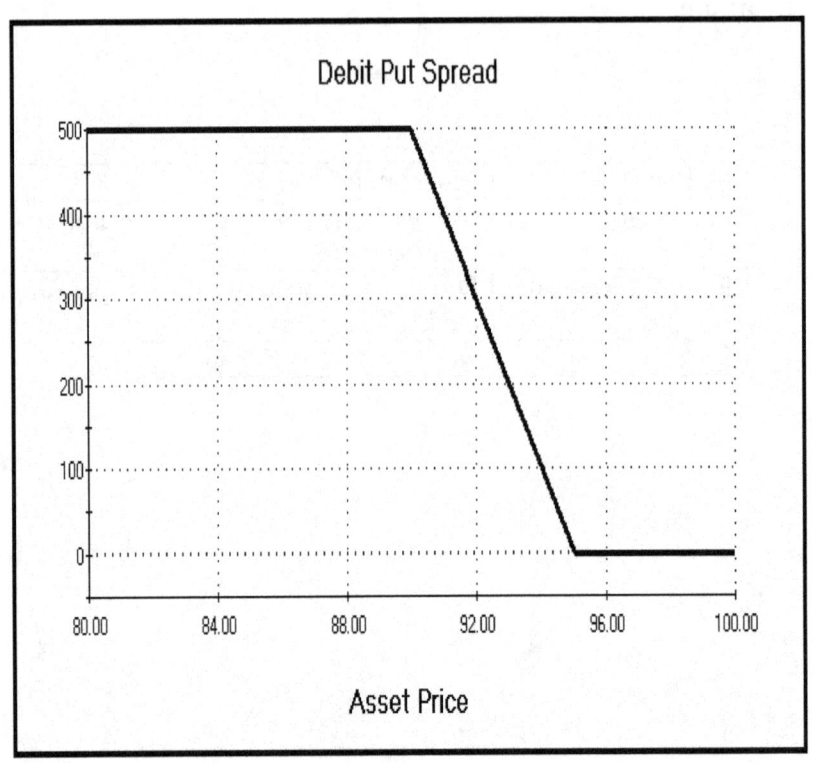

Debit Put Spread

This strategy involves the purchase of one or more puts and the sale of an equal number of puts with a lower strike price. In case of a fall in the asset price, the long leg must be able to create a profit greater than the loss on the short leg. On the other hand, in case of a rise in the asset price, the net premium paid for the spread would be a smaller loss than a long put alone.

Market Bias	Moderately Bullish
Risk	Net premium paid (debit)
Potential Reward	Difference in strike prices; less premium paid
Premium	Net premium paid at purchase; not subject to further margin calls

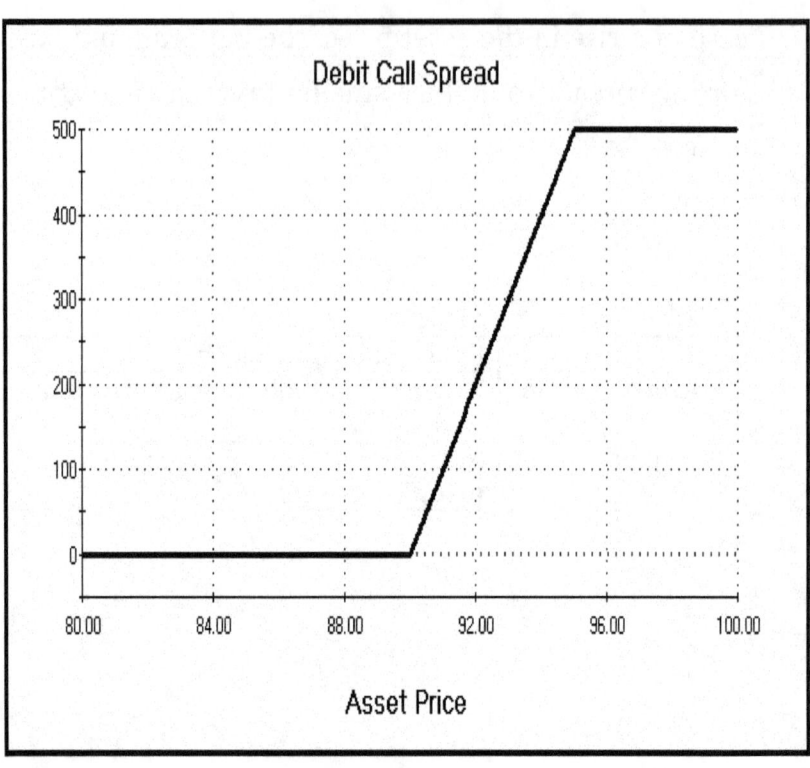

Conclusion

Hopefully, this book has served its purpose- educating the beginner in the art of trading options. A word of caution must be emphasized; however, that the trade of options is as much a dangerous sphere for the unprepared trader as it is a gold mine for the prepared trader. Options provide a unique avenue into the sphere of trade and opens up the path to understanding not only the options market, but the categories underlying which include stock, futures and the various forms of financial instruments including bonds.

The options market is a good place to start for potential long term traders, hopefully this book serves the purpose of enlightening the reader and not only so, but inspiring trade as well. Good luck in your journey to wealth!